ENRICHING THE CURRICULUM WITH CURRENT EVENTS

LILLIAN C. HOWITT

principal, public school 145
formerly assistant principal
winthrop junior high school, brooklyn, new york

TEACHERS PRACTICAL PRESS, INC.

Robert L. Schain, Editor-in-Chief
Murray Polner, Associate Editor

The TEACHERS PRACTICAL PRESS, INC. subscribes to the philosophy that the key to good teaching is to be found in the quality of the teacher himself. This being the case, we recognize the great value and need for today's educator to develop and maintain a continuing program of professional self-improvement through the acquisition of up-to-date teaching techniques. This practical help can be gained only by becoming knowledgeable about practices and methods which have been found useful and successful.

Our goal is to provide this vital area of practical information for all educators. We hope that our series will contribute to the improvement of the teacher and teaching.

Library of Congress Catalog Card Number: 63-14811

CONTENTS

3

1

PREPARATIONS FOR CURRENT EVENTS STUDY

▶ The first lesson

The first lesson should be a discussion of the topic, "Why should we study this subject?" or "Why is this subject required by our city and state as part of our school curriculum?" These topics are so important as a frame of reference and as a guide to what should be taken up that very often more than one lesson may be devoted to this discussion. The following points, among others, may be discussed and stressed with *practical, current, personal* references to illustrate them:

A. To UNDERSTAND THE PRESENT:

Use headlines in a newspaper. What are our problems today? What past events created the world we live in? In addition, such questions as the following may be asked in a *social studies* lesson:

"Why do you attend a school in the United States and not elsewhere?"

"Why do we speak English and not French or German?"

"Why did your ancestors leave the old country?"

"How would your life be different had they not come here?"

"Why do we have a president and not a king or queen, although we are very fond of Queen Elizabeth II of England?"

History will give us the answer explaining how we are as we are today.

In the *mathematics* lesson the following questions may be asked:

"How are you able to compute your school average? How do you compute the batting average of one of the National League players?"

"Your father reads the stock market page. How can he determine how much his stocks have gone up?"

"The government has recently declared an increase in the sales tax, the gasoline tax. How much more will you have to spend with each 10-dollar purchase?"

"The most recent addition to the social security law explains what percent of your salary will go to the social security fund. How will you determine your take home pay?"

"The government has announced a deficit of —— dollars. What does that mean to you?"

What is the conclusion? Mathematics will explain how current events affect us directly.

In the *science* lesson the following questions may be asked:

"Newspapers write about thermonuclear explosions. What does that mean to you?"

"There was an epidemic of smallpox recently in the news. Why is this an unusual news item today?"

"How is it possible for a jet to travel so quickly? How has your life been different because of the changes in transportation? In communications?"

"Why is it that our average life span today in the United States is nearly 70 years compared with about 30 years for people in the Middle East?"

"Why are you able to have strawberries in January?"

Conclusion: Science will help you understand how our lives have been prolonged and made more comfortable for us today.

B. COME TO A CONCLUSION AND FORMULATE OPINIONS:

This topic is basic for lessons in English and science, as well as social studies. The class may be asked questions such as the following in a social studies class: "Which system of government do you favor, the American or the system used in Britain with a queen as its head?" Invariably the children will favor the American system and oppose the British system but will fail to understand the *why* of the answer.

How shall we find out? "If you had an opportunity to vote, whom would you choose? Why or why not? How shall we find out?"

In a science class, the following questions might be asked: "Do you believe the world is round? How do you know? How shall we find out?" "Is there enough food in the world to supply all the people? On what do you base your answer?" "Is fluoridation of water good for our health? How shall we find out?"

6

C. To Understand Our Rights and Duties as Citizens:

The children may be asked, "Is there any policy of our government with which you are dissatisfied? What can you as a citizen under twenty-one do about it?"

D. To Learn How to Carry on a Discussion:

To disagree amicably without offending or interfering with the right of others to present their point of view is essential in a free society. "Why should we hear all points of view?"
Conclusion: Why should we study this subject?

Thus, in the development of the aims and objectives of any subject constant reference will be made to the need for understanding the present and to the importance of studying many possible solutions to our problems.

▶ *The second lesson*

The second lesson should deal with the scope of the term's work. The teacher, by careful questioning, will guide the children in determining the topics to be discussed for the term, with the aims of the specific curriculum kept clearly in mind. The *class* will help to determine the topics and types of facts to be stressed. Here again, the daily newspaper headings, cartoons, and pictures of current weekly magazines are excellent devices in guiding pupils. References should be made to economic, political, or social problems for which the pupils are seeking an explanation or possible solution. For example, if the curriculum deals with American history from colonial times to the Civil War (grades 5-8 or 11) the following news items and current happenings lead the class to give the pertinent topics to be discussed during the year:

Current Articles	Topics to be Studied
Immigrants, Refugees:	Period of Colonization
Cold War:	Policy of Isolation
Desegregation:	Slavery and the Civil War
Civil Rights Headlines:	Contributions to Democracy in Colonial Days; Study of the Constitution
Alaska, Hawaii or Western States:	Territorial Expansion
Outer-Space Discoveries:	Period of Exploration and Discovery

7

In science lessons in any grade, the following news items could lead the class to determine which pertinent units of work should be discussed during the year in the science course:

Current Article	Unit to be Studied
Typhoid epidemic in a Swiss town:	How we can secure and maintain good health
Population Explosion: New items	How does man get his food?
Transportation today: Planes, boats, automobiles, etc.	What makes things move?
Space articles dealing with our "Space" age:	What is our planetary system like? What is air?
Fires in the news:	What causes fires? What are sources of heat and energy?

Thus, the teacher should lead the class to the conclusion that every topic to be discussed in the course of the term is related in some way to the present.

▶ The third lesson

The third lesson should revolve around this topic: "How shall we go about achieving our aims within the scope of the term's work?" This lesson is one in which the class should receive training in the use of the text, newspapers, current periodicals, and other learning aids. A practical approach is necessary here. Children should bring newspapers to school and the teacher should direct them to the proper use of the paper: headlines, index, pictures, cartoons, etc. (*See* Chapter 2.) The same could be done with weekly periodicals. Thus, the class is introduced to sources of information on topics of current interest, newspapers and weekly magazines. At the same time they are led to see the importance of integrating them with the text. With the average young pupil, the weekly magazine serves as an excellent summary and background for newspaper articles which are more difficult for him to understand. An important reminder: Merely telling pupils that reading newspapers and current periodicals is important is not enough. The lesson must be presented *concretely with copies of newspapers and magazines as illustrative materials* used by the teacher in the classroom.

2

SELECTING AND USING NEWSPAPERS AND CURRENT PERIODICALS

It is quite understandable that children in the primary grades, one through three, are not ready to read newspapers. However, they should be introduced to periodicals, e.g., *My Weekly Reader,* in order to prepare them for the more difficult reading materials, newspapers, in the upper grades in elementary school.

Therefore, this topic should constitute a series of lessons to be taken up at the beginning of the school year. This topic is particularly important to pupils in all grades from the fifth year up through the secondary school level since pupils at this level are ready to read newspapers. When we see how avidly our youngsters turn to newspapers to read the "sports" page or other special features of a newspaper, we realize that they can read a newspaper if they are properly motivated and properly directed. The following questions should be fully discussed with practical examples used by the teacher in the lesson:

1. Why are newspapers important to a democratic system?
2. What services do our newspapers offer us today?
3. How shall we select the newspaper we should read?
4. How do we go about reading a newspaper?
5. How can we distinguish fact from opinion in a newspaper?
6. How can we relate our work in class with our daily reading of the newspaper?

The following are a series of lessons which were presented to pupils of varying abilities in the upper grades in the elementary schools and to students on the secondary school level.[1] They were

---

[1] Prepared by Sherry Landsman, Winthrop Junior High School, Brooklyn, New York.

worked out with references to current situations of interest to the students in a particular community. The important features to keep in mind in the development of these lessons are:

1. The class must actually handle a newspaper while the lesson is being developed.
2. The teacher should study the newspapers to make sure that she refers to articles of interest to the particular class she is teaching. This is the basis of her motivation—personal, real experiences.
3. Throughout the term daily references should be made to the newspaper, relating daily lessons to the events in the world around us.

► Three newspaper lessons for language arts and social studies classes

(*Note:* With some classes, this will extend over more than one period.)

Lesson I

Aim: Why do we read newspapers? Which newspapers should we read to get the greatest benefits from our "free press"?

Material: Pupils in each row are to bring into class a daily newspaper as follows: Row 1—The *Daily News;* Row 2—*The New York Times;* Row 3—The *Herald Tribune;* Row 4—*New York Post;* Row 5—*New York World Telegram;* Row 6—*New York Journal American.* (*Note:* Teachers will, of course, assign newspapers from their own localities; there should be, if possible, a representation of tabloids, morning papers, evening papers, etc.)

Motivation: The World Series is on this week. If you wanted to know what is going on, where would you look for such information? Why?

Outline:

    I. Reasons for reading a newspaper
       A. To get information about the city, nation, world
       B. For amusement: puzzles, comics, etc.
       C. For advertisements
       D. For opinions
       E. For employment
       F. For excitement
    II. To what extent our city papers carry out these functions

10

III. Evaluation of our city papers

Development:
    I. Why do you or your parents read a newspaper?
       A. To learn about our city, nation, and the world.

          Medial Summary: Many of us have relatives who are being called back to the service.

              Why should we be particularly interested in reading the newspaper?

              Today, in our city, we have a particular interest in reading the papers. Why?

              Use other examples relating to national, city, and foreign affairs.

          Application: What is one thing you will look for in a newspaper to make that paper your choice?

       B. When I take the paper home, my son and his friends seem to have a special interest in rushing to get it first. Why?

          Medial Summary: What is the second feature you might be interested in getting from your paper?

       C. It seems that wives and daughters also have a very personal interest in reading the newspaper for reasons other than those indicated. Explain.
       D. We are particularly interested in the editorial page of the newspaper. Why?
       E. Discuss other reasons why people read newspapers.

Summary: Of all the services rendered, which do you think is most important?

Application: If all newspapers, magazines, etc., would suddenly stop operating, what would be the results to you?

Lesson II

Review: What are the chief purposes of reading a newspaper?

Aim: To what extent does each newspaper carry out the functions discussed?

Material: Pupils in each row are to bring into class a daily newspaper as follows: Row 1—A morning paper; Row 2—An afternoon paper; Row 3—A local paper; Row 4—An out of town paper; Row 5—A tabloid.

(*Note:* Try to obtain as many different kinds of newspapers as possible, e.g., daily, weekly, state-wide, national, etc.)

Procedure: The lesson will become a counting lesson as follows: Look at your paper and count the pages devoted to news— national, international, city scandal, special features and amusements, advertisements, business, editorial, pictures.

Conclusions:
1. What does each newspaper seem to specialize in?
2. In view of the discussion on topic I, which newspapers should we read?
3. Why then do people often read a number of newspapers?

Application:
1. Read the radio advertisement concerning *The New York Times:* Why do they call it a "newspaper for people who think"?
2. If your father were a stock investor, what newspaper should he read?
3. As an elementary school student—which newspaper? a junior high school student? a high school student?
4. If you are in a hurry to get a quick picture of the news, which newspaper would you read? Explain. What danger is there in getting the news in this manner?
5. If you are interested in sports which paper would you use? If you are interested in books and the theater? Advertisements?

Final Conclusion: Which newspaper seems to carry a combination of all these services?

Lesson III

Aim: How to read a newspaper.

Material: The lesson may be taught by having all students bring to class the same paper. For further development a few children may have copies of different papers.

Motivation: What does the headline mean to you?

Development:
I. Headline: How to get news quickly
   A. Why are some headlines larger than others?
   B. Why were there so many different interpretations of the headlines?
   C. Where can we find out what really happened? (The importance of the right column)

12

D. Read the right column. How does it compare with the ideas you had about the headline?

Medial Summary: Compare headlines in different papers

Conclusion: What is the danger of just reading headlines?

II. Pictures in the paper. (Proceed as above emphasizing the danger of the influence of pictures on the emotions of the reader.)

III. Important facts in the news

A. Where shall we find the most important facts in the news?

B. Compare the articles on page 1 with those on page 31.

C. How can facts be hidden? (Refer to headlines, location of articles, omissions.)

D. Do advertisements affect the presentation of facts in the news? (Refer to advertisements relating to smoking, drugs, foods, etc.)

E. Compare the amount of space given in the . . . . . . newspaper with the amount of space in the . . . . . . paper on topics such as, "Pure Foods Act," "Smoking," "Labor Disputes," etc.

F. Where do newspapers get their information? How does that influence the presentation of the facts? (This is an enrichment question for bright classes.)

Medial Summary: Why was it important for us to discuss this topic?

IV. Opinions in the newspaper

A. How do newspapers reveal their opinions on important issues?

B. Should we read newspapers which have your opinions only? Explain.

Final Summary and Drill: What part of the paper will you read to get:

1. The news, quickly?
2. Your paper's opinion on important events?
3. The opinion of readers?
4. An explanation of a headline?

Application: How can our papers be improved to insure the best possible press?

The following constitutes a series of lessons which aim to "de-velop the ability to use the imagination and the environment as a resource for creative expression." These lessons utilize local color as a basis for art. The artist becomes a reporter of world affairs by utilizing color, design, line, and visual imagery to amplify the printed word describing world events.

▶ Newspapers in art classes: grades 5-12

Aim: The artist is a recorder of life around him.
Motivation:

    a) In the year 1700, how large was a person's local com-munity? How large is our community today? How has our conception of our world or neighborhood today in-creased or grown because of communication; i.e., news-papers, television and transportation?

    b) Where does an artist obtain his ideas? If our artist gets his ideas from the world around him, why in our "mod-ern day and age" has the whole world become the artist's neighborhood?

    c) Can you think of any scenes that are recorded in your newspaper or television which have become familiar to you?

    d) Open your newspapers and choose a local, national, or international headline which you could illustrate not only as an artist but as a reader of current events. Ex-amples: "Thousands Turn Out for Spring in the Park," (Park scene), "U.N. Guides Enjoy Challenge of Jobs," (U.N. Scene), "Nuclear Submarine Christened," (Naval Yard Scene), "Fire at . . . .," (Fire Fighting), "Slum Clearance Continues," (Building Scene for chil-dren who cannot draw figures), "Mrs. Kennedy Tours India," (Color and Costumes), "U.A.R. and Israel Test U.N. Peace Efforts," (Border patrol crowd scenes), etc.

Pivotal Points:

    1. A discussion of the qualities of the environment that would interest the artist: What characteristics would you find in the environment indicated by your headline? Would they be: a. drabness b. color c. activity d. serenity e. noise f. space g. people h. buildings i. street objects?

14

2. How would the artist re-create the atmosphere of "local color"?
   a. What method had the reporter used to indicate "local color"? Adjectives. What are the adjectives of art? Line and color.
3. Utilization of charts: Color suggests noise, excitement, serenity, drabness. Bright colors suggest noise, excitement; dull colors suggest quiet and drabness. Use an association game to bring out these ideas.
4. How does line suggest moods? Look at these drawings of a tree. Which tree is gay? Which is violent? What has the artist used to suggest these moods? (He used lines.) Develop:
   a. Straight lines suggest serenity.
   b. Curved lines suggest gaiety.
   c. Slanted lines suggest violence.

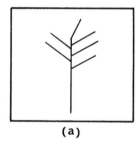

(a)

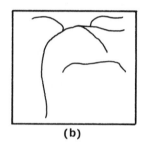

(b)

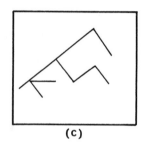

(c)

5. Reporters often try to influence their readers by presenting their point of view. How can you as an artist give your point of view? Look at these two pictures of the same scene. How have they indicated their point of view? (Use pictures showing the use of perspective and placement for emphasis.)

Development:
   A. Choose your headline. Block in your figures, shapes, and forms. Choose the correct line and color to suggest the mood of your news story. Ask yourselves the following questions just as a reporter asks questions when he writes a current events story: Who, what, when, where, how?
   B. Pivotal Questions:
      1. Where would you place yourself in relation to the setting? Would you be:

15

a. close to it
b. next to it
c. to one side

d. above it
e. far away
f. on the same level
g. part of it

2. How would you place your figures in relation to your point of view?
3. What part of your picture would you emphasize? How would you emphasize it?
4. What line would you choose to indicate the mood of your picture: excitement, serenity, noise, or drabness? Describe the kind of lines you would use: diagonal, straight or curved?
5. What colors would you use to illustrate the mood of your story?

C. Key Words—placement, emphasis, mood, line and color.
D. Materials: Tempera paint, chalk, 19x22 paper, brushes.

Summary: Why may an artist be called an historian? What have these international or national artists said about their environment? How have they used line and color to suggest their point of view? How have you used line and color to suggest your point of view?

Evaluation: (Of pupil's work)
1. Which painting suggests atmosphere and mood? How have they suggested the mood?
2. Which painting shows great powers of observation? of memory?
3. Which paintings have an interesting design quality? Why?
4. Which painting conveys a visual or emotional reaction through perspective? through the ways in which the medium was handled? How has this been done?
5. Which artists have created local, national, and international scenes which are familiar to us?

Application:
1. How have such magazines as *Life* and *Look* become recorders of history?
2. Choose a scene from your everyday experience or from the newspaper and illustrate this event from your particular point of view.
3. Write your experience as a newspaper article and illus-

16

trate your story. (This can be done in cooperation with the language arts and social studies teachers.)

Because of the importance of developing a newspaper reading habit, a habit of reading about the vital news in the world around us, these lessons should be taken up at the beginning of each school year with varying modifications depending on the age, maturity, and ability of the class.

▶ Using periodicals

In many classes, there are pupils who are not quite ready to read newspapers on a regular, daily basis, because their reading ability is not developed or because they lack a proper factual background to enable them to understand the news. A weekly periodical is very important as a way of preparing these groups for daily reading of a newspaper. However, to be most effective, the use of such periodicals must be related to the daily newspaper. Otherwise there will be no transition to the habit of reading a daily paper.

Teachers of social studies have found the following periodicals helpful in their classes:

Grades 1-3	*My Weekly Reader* (American Education Publications, 1250 Fairwood Avenue, Columbus 16, Ohio)
Grades 5-6	*Current Events, Junior Review*
Grades 7-9	*Junior Review* (Slow groups)
Grades 7-8	*Junior Scholastic* (50 West 44th Street, New York City)
Grade 9	*World Week* (50 West 44th Street, New York City)
Grades 10-12	*Senior Scholastic* (50 West 44th Street, New York City)
Grade 6	*World Week* (Intellectually gifted)

Teachers of science have found the following periodicals helpful in their classes:

Grades 1-4	*My Weekly Reader* (American Education Publications, 1250 Fairwood Avenue, Columbus 16, Ohio)
Grades 5-10	*Current Science* (American Education Publications, 1250 Fairwood Avenue, Columbus 16, Ohio)
Grades 7-10	*Science Newsletter* (for special reports) (Science Service, Inc., 1719 N Street, N.W., Washington 6, D.C.)

3

INTRODUCING OTHER MEDIA

▶ **Basic classroom displays**

A classroom should have a picture of the various activities in which pupils are currently engaged. Some of these activities may represent "on-going" projects for the entire term. Still others may indicate a special study of even shorter duration, the study of a specific topic or significant news item. Others may represent materials to be used for future work. Such displays would be functional. They should be useful to the children to help them learn; they should be utilized in the classroom to help develop specific concepts or skills.

Such displays should not be confined entirely within the classroom. Every school should have an exciting, colorful hall display dealing with an important current happening. The responsibility for such displays should be rotated among the classes and should be changed approximately every two weeks. With Africa in the news in recent years, one of the most interesting displays which aroused interest in the school's student body was a display on Africa, its geography, culture, and rising nationalist movements, prepared by pupils in art classes. Such a display included costumes, scenes of Africa showing the "old" Africa mingling with the "new" Africa—colorful market places and super-markets, jungle-clad natives and modern voting scenes, interesting faces, group scenes, landscapes showing tropical growths, all telling the story of changing Africa.

The following are some ideas which not only may be used as functional displays but which suggest specific teaching techniques: [1]

---

[1] Prepared by Barney Yukolis, Winthrop Junior High School, Brooklyn, New York.

▶ Current events bulletin board

Some General Rules About Bulletin Boards

DO—Provide a heading for the bulletin board.
> Avoid clutter.
> Use headlines and subheadlines.
> Underline, in red, key sentences when posting news items.
> Use a variety of current sources: many different newspapers, magazines, etc.
> Use at least one appropriate question related to the articles posted.
> Organize the items under topics.
> Make the board simple and attractive.
> Vary the display regularly.
> Utilize pupils' help in preparing displays.

DO NOT—Use long detailed articles.
> Post whole magazines.
> Display news items which have lost their timeliness.
> Display news items which are not referred to in class.

The following are some suggestions for a current events bulletin board. Use this as a heading: WE WANT TO LEARN WHAT IS HAPPENING IN THE WORLD AROUND US.

Newspaper articles should be displayed under these permanent headings:

ASIA	AMERICA	LOCAL	EUROPE
Articles	Articles	Articles	Articles

A similar bulletin board could be made by utilizing pictures taken from newspapers instead of articles. Another bulletin board could be made by utilizing maps.

A simple map of the world, clearly showing all the continents, could be permanently displayed. Attach to each continent a colored ribbon. At the other end of each ribbon, a brief news item, headline, or summary of an important news article of the week pertaining to that area could be attached. These news items should be changed weekly. This procedure is not only attractive but it also gives the class an opportunity to learn geography in connection with current happenings.

Another bulletin board could be labeled, *BEFORE AND AFTER*. Many topics lend themselves to a study of "Before" and "After." Such ideas may be depicted on a chart which could "grow" as the topic develops. It may also be used as the application step of a unit of study. The following topics may be depicted in this manner:

Health:	Epidemics During the Middle Ages	Epidemics in the 20th Century
Transportation: (Sea, air)	Before 20th Century	During 20th Century
Communication:	Signals	Wireless
The Theatre:	Ancient Greece	Broadway
Industrial Developments:		
Use of Power	Animal Power	Atomic Power
Methods of Production	Hand Labor	Belt System
Agricultural Developments:	Crop Rotation	Use of Fertilizers
Number Systems:	Egyptian Binary System	Modern Decimal System
Measurements:	Ancient Rome	Today
Musical Instruments:	Medieval Days	Modern
Housing Conditions:	Before	Now

"WE SEE BOTH SIDES OF THE STORY" is another suggestion for a heading on a current events bulletin board. It is one of the aims of all teachers that our pupils learn, very early in their schooling, the ability to suspend judgments and to see both sides of a story. When any controversial topic is taken up, a chart or some other visual aid should be used, particularly with younger children, to focus attention on the fact that there is more than one side to a story, that conclusions and judgments be suspended until both sides are heard.

SPECIAL VOCABULARY WE SHOULD KNOW RELATING TO OUR SUBJECT. This is an "on-going" type of bulletin board which grows as the term advances.

Science Vocabulary	Definition	Examples from Our Daily Lives
Compound	Two or more elements	Water: combined elements: oxygen and hydrogen
Control	combined with each	
Kindling Point	other	
Element		
Microbe		

Mathematics Vocabulary	Definition	Examples from Our Daily Lives
Mixed number	The sum of a whole number and a fraction	1½ pounds of cherries
Quotient		
Multiplier		
Decade		
Fractional Part		

Social Studies Vocabulary	Definition	Examples from Our Daily Lives
Political	Relating to government	Voting in an election
Social		
Economic		
Democracy		
Dictatorship		

HISTORY AFFECTS OUR LIVES TODAY would be a very important growing bulletin board which will help the class see relationships between past events and our life today. For example:

What Happened	Effects on Us
1. Revolutionary War	A free United States
2. Amendment XIII	All men are free
3. Quartering Act	Amendment III, U.S. Constitution

or

Scientific Discoveries	
1. Discovery of the atom	Atomic power for peacetime uses
2. Pasteurization	Purification of milk
3. Mechanical advantage	Machines which make work easier for us: the pulley, the propellor

▶ We learn by studying maps

Newspapers, magazines and periodicals usually have maps which give at a glance the current news. This is quite useful in science, social studies, and mathematics classes. *Scholastic Magazine* and *Newsweek* provide excellent maps which can be used for such displays. For lower grades, *My Weekly Reader* has very interesting colorful maps for classroom use.

▶ We learn from radio and TV broadcasts

This may be used as a heading for a chart to direct children's attention to current programs on the air. This chart should be kept up to date.

<u>WE LEARN FROM READING CARTOONS</u>. Cartoons are excellent devices for learning current events. They are concrete visual aids, usually amusing, and a good means of motivating interest. Often a current cartoon may be used to fit a topic in history being discussed in class by asking the students to change the words. For example, a common cartoon of today is one which represents a "delicate balancing act to maintain peace today." The words could be changed to apply to the Civil War or the World Wars. In a science class, the same cartoon can be changed to "Uses of Atomic Power in Industry." In a mathematics class, the words can be changed to figures relating to money spent for education and science among the western powers as compared with the sums spent for this purpose in the U.S.S.R. and her satellites.

▶ Preparing display files

Such displays when integrated with daily lessons make any subject real, concrete, and current. Teachers should, therefore, try to build up files of current pictures, charts, and cartoons to be used as a basis for future lessons. Monitorial squads should be trained to keep these displays up-to-date and attractive. A filing system of such displays should be arranged topically to be used in the classroom for motivation, development, and summarization of lessons. Such material may easily be stored in properly labeled folders. Each term folders should be carefully examined to keep the visual aids current and meaningful.

▶ Other non-reading resources

1. Filmstrips, films, tapes, and recordings should be previewed by the teacher. It is suggested that a summary be made of such aids organized by grades and topics. There should be a periodic reappraisal of such visual aids to make sure they are up-to-date.

2. The opaque projector and the overhead projector are two excellent tools to use when discussing a flat picture. They enable all pupils to see cartoons, pictures, headlines, and charts clearly.

3. Realia and artifacts are very useful. Students should be encouraged to bring such materials to school.

4. Community trips and the use of guest speakers should not be overlooked. In the lower grades, a trip to a depot or a fruit market is a method of teaching about current happenings related to "Food" or "World Trade." In the upper grades, speakers from a local news-

paper or a representative of a foreign country will help make the present more meaningful.

In all cases involving the use of non-reading media, the teacher must keep in mind:

1. Careful training of the class in listening and observing.
2. Preparation of the class *before* the presentation of a program or a trip.
3. Training of the class in proper procedures *during* the listening or viewing period.
4. Preparation of follow-up procedures *after* the program is presented.

Radio News Broadcast

Aim: Which news broadcast should we listen to? [2]

Motivation: Assume that you are snow-bound for a short period of time.

How can you keep up with what is happening in the world?

Materials: Tape Recorder, Two 15 minute News Broadcasts

Development:

A. Directed Listening—(1) Draw three columns on a sheet of paper (2) Label each column, local, national, and international respectively (3) Classify each item you hear into one of these groups by placing the main idea in the appropriate column.

B. Pivotal Questions
1. What do we want to learn about different broadcasts?
2. Why do you listen to the A.M. broadcast? To the P.M. broadcast?
3. What type of news is emphasized on each broadcast?
4. Which group does each broadcast try to reach? Explain.

Content Outline:

I. Type of news broadcasts
A. A.M.   C. 15 minutes
B. P.M.   D. 5 minutes
II. Type of news on a broadcast
III. Audience reached by each broadcast
IV. Conclusions

Summary: Which of these two broadcasts would you listen to? Why?

Application: 1. Why do you find you still have to read newspapers?
2. What is the difference between a news broadcast and a newspaper?

---

[2] Presented by Florence Berman, P.S. 175, Brooklyn, N.Y., to a 5th grade class.

The Radio and Television Broadcasts in the Primary Grades: 1-3. Children in the primary grades may be asked to report on specific radio and television programs as part of their homework assignment. Of course, the parent is usually asked to cooperate. These youngsters can be asked to identify some personality in the news whose picture they saw in class. This is often done during election campaigns. This device might be used to familiarize children with the picture and voice of the President of the United States or of other prominent officials. It might be used to enable children to become familiar with places important in the news: a picture of the White House, Congress, etc. Children may be asked to watch programs describing a special event: Thanksgiving Day, Washington's Birthday, Veteran's Day, etc.

Radio and Television Broadcasts for Classes in Grades 4-6. Older children could report on what they see and hear. Sometimes such lessons may be used to motivate children to read newspapers. Since young children have difficulty in selecting articles to read in the newspaper, they are able to narrow their choice by restricting it to those topics discussed on the 8 A.M. or 9 A.M. broadcast. While the class is listening to such broadcasts, the topics are written in a list on the chalkboard. Pupils then copy this list into their notebooks for homework, and find these articles in the newspaper. These articles are discussed in class the next day. The students read headlines and subtitles, they name the important personalities involved in the news, and give a summary of the news events. Pupils are asked to locate places on the world map. Any historical parallels can be introduced at the time. Finally, an experience chart of the most important article of the day is made by the class as a conclusion to this lesson.

4

HOW TO MAKE USE
OF SPECIAL EVENTS

This chapter will include many suggestions for bringing current events into the classroom when a special occasion warrants it.

Suggestions below will be classified according to subject areas. However, each subject teacher should aim to articulate and integrate her work with all other areas in the curriculum. For example: *mathematics*—interpretation of charts and graphs dealing with current issues; *science*—lessons on racial differences, heredity, and contributions made by all nationalities; *English*—editorials and dramatizations of historical events or plays on Brotherhood; *home economics*—fashion shows and Food Festivals dealing with "Foods and Dress of Many Lands."

▶ Brotherhood: understanding human relations

The following is a list of suggestions which might be helpful in planning lessons which will emphasize and build good human relationships. Pivotal questions which may be used in teaching a unit on any specific nationality are the following:

1. How has the culture of the nationality contributed to our way of life—shelter, food, clothing, science?
2. How did the geography of the_____nationality affect its living conditions?
3. How have we influenced or changed the culture of this nation or nationality?
4. How is the country of the_____nationality governed? How does their system of government affect the life of the people?

5. What have we taken from the culture of these people in the way of art, literature, language, science, sports, entertainment, fashions, defense?
6. How can we express Brotherhood in a dynamic, active way?
7. What opportunities exist in our school to develop a feeling of Brotherhood?
   a. How do pooling resources when working on a unit help feeling of Brotherhood?
   b. How can problem-solving procedures help create a feeling of Brotherhood?
   c. How do our club programs help promote Brotherhood?
   d. How do our assembly programs promote Brotherhood?
   e. How does our General Organization help promote Brotherhood?
   f. How does our community center help promote Brotherhood?

SPECIAL PROJECTS OR ACTIVITIES FOR ANY SUBJECT AREA

1. The teacher could invite a parent to talk on how she lived in her native land.
2. Foreign-born children in the class could describe a typical day spent in their old country.
3. Map project: America—A Nation of One People from Many Countries or a Nation of Many People from Many Countries.
4. Special Projects: Who Is Building Our New School? Interview people connected with the renovation of our school: principal, engineers, foreman, workers, and others. Get the following information from each person interviewed:

   Nationality
   Nature of his work
   The importance of each job to the total job
   The part played by each nationality in helping to get us a new building.

5. Develop a "Did You Know?" corner for each nationality studied, indicating interesting facts about this nationality.
6. Develop a local "Who's Who" showing the part played by members of a minority group in the community. Develop a "Who's Who" of the graduates of your school from minority groups.

1. How other nationalities have influenced American popular music.
2. How other nationalities have influenced our modern dances.
3. Folk songs and folk dances of many lands which are popular in America.

UNITS IN SCIENCE

1. A unit on the concept of race and nationality. (Great care should be exercised to break down prejudices where they do exist, and not to create prejudices where none exist.)
   a. What is a race? What is a nationality?
   b. Common misunderstandings.
      1. A man's hereditary features and his race.
      2. His language and his race.
      3. His culture and his race.
2. A study of the nationality of the scientists who influenced our lives in the following fields: Medicine, conquest of space, development of power resources, improvement in transportation and communications, developments in industry—synthetics.
3. Genetics and inherited traits of character.
4. A unit on the topic: "All races today are mongrel."

SOCIAL STUDIES

1. Geography lesson: How geographic features were responsible for creating differences among people.
   a. How different food habits have developed because of different geographic factors. *New England*—sea food; *China*—rice; *American Indian*—corn.
   b. How isolated areas, areas with poor transportation were influential. *Amazon jungle; Jungles of Africa.*
   c. How droughts and the lack of adequate resources affect people of a nation. *Irish* in the nineteenth century; *Italians* in the nineteenth century; peoples of *Southeast Asia.*
2. How government policies are responsible for creating differences among people.
   a. European ghettos and their effect on the Jewish people involved.
   b. Educational policies. United States and American Literacy; czarist Russia—Illiteracy of Russian immigrants,

1900-20; Nineteenth century Italy—Illiteracy of the Italians, 1900-20; education of the Southern Negro today.
3. Population Movements and Trends.
   a. Current events will serve as a basis for this topic. Refugees from Eastern to Western Zone of Germany; movement of Puerto Ricans to the United States.
   b. Reasons for such migrations today. These should be compared with reasons for migrations in the past.
   c. Influence of the new environment on the immigrant.
   d. Influence of the immigrant on the new environment.
   e. Migration within the United States.
4. A unit on income and standards of living and their effects on the economic, social and cultural lives of the people.
5. Who built our railroads and canals?
   Unit—People of all nationalities can advance when given an opportunity—survey of people in the neighborhood who have "made good."

Language Arts

1. Unit on prejudice.
   a. What is meant by the term, "Prejudice"?
   b. How can we detect prejudices in this country?
2. Housing and crime: Relationship between environment and crime is to be stressed.
3. A unit on the population of the United States: Our Heterogeneous Population.
4. International school correspondence.
   a. Junior Red Cross Correspondence Program.
   b. United Nations.
   c. International Friendship League.
   d. Pen Pals.
   e. Draw up a list of other organizations or nations to suit the need of your class.
5. Write a special column in the school newspaper on the culture of a different nationality for each issue.

Sources of Information

1. National Council for Social Studies, 1201 16th Street, N.W., Washington, D. C.
2. B'nai B'rith, 3212 Coney Island Avenue, Brooklyn, N. Y.
3. National Council of Christians and Jews, 105 Court St., Brooklyn, N. Y.
4. New York State Commission on Discrimination in Housing, 35 West 32 Street, New York, N. Y.

5. National Association for the Advancement of Colored People, 169 Fifth Ave., New York, N. Y.
6. Council Against Intolerance, Lincoln Building, New York, N. Y.
7. Pan American Student League, Washington, D. C.
8. *La Prensa,* 245 Canal Street, New York, N. Y.
9. New York State Commission Against Discrimination, 270 Broadway, New York, N. Y.

▶ Election—America's big political event

Fewer than 60% of those eligible to vote actually voted in most of our elections. Not only do we want an interested citizenry, but one which can vote intelligently. The challenge to teachers of social studies is to impress children with the seriousness of their active participation in government long before they are of voting age. The election is an excellent opportunity for the social studies teacher to keep alive interest in politics which this event usually arouses even in our youngsters. The following are some suggestions which may be used and which, we hope, might help us build capable, active citizens. Please note that the interest and activities should not end with election day. Follow-up events are important to keep the children politically alert and interested. (*Note:* These suggestions may be modified to suit any grade level from grade one through grade twelve.)

Word Study

primary	convention	party	electoral
majority	plurality	platform	college
proposition	balloting	dark horse	band wagon
incumbent	"off-year"	caucus	floor leader
ticket	election	patronage	pivotal state
		inauguration	

ELECTION FACTS

- The electoral college—winner take all
- Parties: Political parties in the United States: organized political teams to arouse the voters
  The battle for the ballot: past and present
  The role of minor parties: past and present
- Nominations: What is a primary, a convention? What happens at our national conventions?
- The voter: Who can vote? It's up to the voters to choose wisely. How?
- Who's who in the coming elections: national, local candidates
- Our vice-presidential candidate: Qualifications, background

29

- Past presidential elections: 1800, 1824, 1860, 1876, 1888, 1932, 1948, 1960
- Party platforms, past and present
- We also elect other candidates in our election: congressional, state, local.

LANGUAGE ARTS

1. Report on special activities in the community.
2. Surveys:
   - 2.1 Neighborhood surveys on past voting records to be reported to the class or to be displayed on graphs or charts.
   - 2.2 Poll of the opinion of the neighborhood on possible outcomes of this election. This may be a block by block poll or a house poll.
3. Writing activities: getting out the vote
   - 3.1 Newspaper editorials on: Why register and vote
   - 3.2 Booklets dealing with the candidates, local and national issues, etc.
   - 3.3 Fact sheets about the current elections to be sent home.
4. Dramatizations:
   - 4.1 Mock election campaigns where pupils summarize political speeches, newspaper statements, etc.
   - 4.2 Organize the class as a national nominating convention.
   - 4.3 Dramatize voting procedures.
   - 4.4 Presenting the candidates to the voters: background, platform, etc.

SOCIAL STUDIES
MAP WORK

1. Make a map of the United States locating the states which have the greatest number of electoral votes. Discuss implications for the candidates, campaign, nominating procedures, platforms, etc.
2. On an outline map or on a map of your own making label the states as follows: R—Republican majority, D—Democratic majority, Dt—Doubtful. Discuss the implications for the campaign.

TEACHING PROCEDURES FOR LANGUAGE ARTS AND SOCIAL STUDIES CLASSES

1. Open Text Work:

A study of our Constitution, Article II; The President.

A study of articles, periodicals and newspapers.

2. Research:

Students could select one or two planks in the platform for special study. Study of background of candidates: Let us look at the past record of our candidates.

3. Debates:

3.1 What stand should our next president take on foreign affairs to help maintain our security?

3.2 Does the convention system of presidential nominations work properly?

3.3 Are campaigns too long and repetitive?

3.4 Should we encourage everyone to vote including those who are unaware of issues and candidates?

Sources of Information

1. *NBC Political Parties and Convention Study Guide,* free to teachers, NBC, 30 Rockefeller Plaza, New York, N. Y.
2. *Participating in Presidential Elections,* student election handbook, Institute of Administrative Research, 525 West 120th St., New York 27, N. Y.
3. *Election Civics,* American Education Publication, 11 West 42nd St., New York 36, N. Y.
4. *Election 1960,* resource guide, free, NEA, 1201 16th St., N.W., Washington 6, D. C.
5. American Heritage Foundation, 11 West 42nd St., New York 36, N. Y.
6. *World Week,* 50 West 44th Street, New York, N. Y.
7. *Current Events Magazine,* "Election Civics," 1960.

Audio-Visual Aids

Electing a President, filmstrip, *New York Times,* a description of the entire election process from the convention to the voting booths, including the powers of the president.

ELECTION DAY LESSON (PRIMARY)

Grade: Bright second year class or average third year class

Motivation: Tomorrow is a holiday. What day do we observe tomorrow?

Show pictures of candidates running for the highest offices.

Lesson:

I. What offices are these people running for?

A. Pretend you are running for president of this class and make a campaign speech.

B. Pretend you are running for head of the (city, state, or nation) and make a campaign speech.

C. Why do candidates running for office make campaign speeches?

II. Voting Procedures
   A. How old must you be to be permitted to vote?
   B. I know people who are twenty-one years of age who cannot vote. Why? What other requirements must a voter meet?
III. Duties of a President (or head of a city, state, or school organization)
   If you were voting for a president, what kind of person would be your choice? Why? What should be some of the duties of the president?

Activities:
1. Discuss officers necessary for the democratic running of a classroom. Make provision for the election of such officers: president, vice-president, secretary, etc. Pupils make campaign speeches. Relate this to national, state or city elections.
2. Take children to see voting machines in the school.
3. Draw pictures showing people going to the polls.
4. Have children bring in a variety of pictures: candidates, candidates campaigning, election results. Display pictures.
5. Assign children to accompany their parents to the polls and report on their experiences.

5

SPECIFIC TECHNIQUES IN CURRENT EVENTS TEACHING

Some of the finest motivations in any subject area or grade level deal with current happenings. However, it is not enough to *introduce* a lesson by referring to a present day event. Such references should be made throughout the lesson culminating in the summary and application step of the lesson. Then, the past becomes real and the present meaningful to our young people. The following outline is a guide to be followed in projecting the present into the past and then back again into the present culminating in anticipating the future. This may be applied to almost any unit of work.

I. Topic.
II. Motivation: A current happening as it relates to the topic for the day.
III. Development of basic facts relating to the topic.
IV. Summary and application steps.
Effects of past events on the present
Comparison of past events with the present
Predictions of future happenings

Since the use of current events as a means of motivating social studies lessons is so basic, the following suggestions for motivating different historical topics should be useful to a teacher:

Many of the motivations listed could be used by teachers for all types of pupils. However, the success in the presentation of any of the motivations listed will often depend on the use of the proper dramatic word or phrase, the tone of voice, the gesture or the proper timing by the teacher. The best motivations are those that can maintain continuous interest in the lesson. Thus, if necessary, there may be a variety of motivations introduced in a lesson at the beginning or the middle and the end of the lesson.

GENERALIZED MOTIVATIONS FOR SOCIAL STUDIES LESSONS

1. Why should we take up this topic?
2. The "we" and "they" approach: We do this . . . . . . while they do that . . . . . .
3. Compile a "Who's Who."
4. Newspaper clipping, preferably pictures, headlines or summaries which shows the relationship between the past and the current situation.
5. Read interesting excerpts from books to be used as a basis for a lesson.
6. Suppose you were a cartoonist for a newspaper. How would you present to your readers a picture of this event?
7. How can you change this modern cartoon to fit the topic we are studying?
8. Draw pictures or cut out pictures which may be projected on an opaque projector. Let the child who contributed the picture explain it to the class.
9. Use a series of cartoons to develop the lesson. Cartoons may be drawn on the board by the teacher or by the children. They may be reproduced and mounted.
10. Utilize the "before" and "after" approach.
11. Utilize socio-drama procedures, role playing and other forms of dramatic presentation.

▶ Motivations: grades 4, 5 and 7, early American history

TOPIC: **Contributions from Colonial Days.** MOTIVATION: Organize a debate, report, editorial, play or cartoon around a topic such as "Our Debt of Gratitude to Our Ancestors." Discuss activities which we engage in today which were handed down from colonial times: sports (bowling), foods, holidays, and so forth.

TOPIC: **Colonization.** MOTIVATION: "Why did your parents, grandparents or other relatives come to America? Let us see if the early colonists came for similar reasons."

TOPIC: **British Colonization.** MOTIVATION: "Why is it that we speak English here, not Spanish or French? Your life and mine would have been different if the Spanish and not the British had

34

control of colonial America. How? Then, how did the British get control of colonial America?"

TOPIC: **Constitutional Convention.** MOTIVATION: Organize a club and compare the procedures with the procedures and problems facing the members at the Constitutional Convention.

TOPIC: **Colonization.** MOTIVATION: Read excerpts from books describing the horrible trials and tribulations of early voyages, for example, Beard, *The Rise of American Civilization;* Huberman, *We, the People.* "Why did people risk such dangers to come to America?" Ask pupils to question a person they know who came to America from another country. This is to be compared with reasons for early colonization.

TOPIC: **Spanish Colonization.** MOTIVATION: "If we were to travel to Puerto Rico or to Mexico, how would we know that the Spanish had settled there?"

TOPIC: **Explorations.** MOTIVATION: Use newspaper articles dealing with explorers today. "Why did people go out on explorations in the past? Why do people go out today?"

TOPIC: **Thomas Jefferson and the Declaration of Independence.** MOTIVATION: "Thomas Jefferson died almost 100 years ago. However, he is still alive today. We must not let him die. Explain this riddle."

TOPIC: **How a Bill Becomes a Law.** MOTIVATION: Utilize a cardboard map of the United States or your state with a slit going through it. Have four forms representing the houses of the legislative branch, the executive branch and the bill. Position accordingly on the map.

► Motivations: all levels, American history in the nineteenth and twentieth centuries

TOPIC: **Civil War.** MOTIVATION: "In fighting a war, what problem does a government face in order to win the war? How did the United States government solve these problems when preparing to fight the Civil War?"

TOPIC: **Assembly Line or Belt System.** MOTIVATION: *Demonstration:* Materials—10 sheets of paper, 10 envelopes. Jobs— a) fill in letter heading, b) fold paper, c) insert in envelope, d) seal envelope, e) address and stamp. Groups of five work this process in the manner of an assembly line. Compare the results with one person doing it by himself.

TOPIC: **Conservation—Natural Resources and Human Resources.** MOTIVATION: Refer to conservation in relation to floods, droughts, scenic areas; refer to vandalism, damage from fires, recent storms, cave-ins, and other natural disasters.

"When you play hard you become worn out. Why? What do you do?"

"Your watch runs down from time to time. Why?"

TOPIC: **Development of the West.** MOTIVATION: Read excerpts from *The Forty-Niners,* by White. Refer to television and motion picture programs.

TOPIC: **Westward Movement.** MOTIVATION: "The United States Government is offering free land and other inducements for people to move to Alaska. Why might we want to go? Why not? Compare with the movement to the West in the nineteenth century."

TOPIC: **Immigration.** MOTIVATION: "From what country did your parents come? Why did they leave?"

▶ Motivations: for any topic in mathematics

1. Why should we take up this topic?
2. The "we" approach: Why is this topic important to us in our daily lives?
3. Find examples in our daily lives where this mathematical procedure or problem may come up. How do we solve it?
4. Find articles in the newspapers, pictures, headlines which show how this unit of work is important in the world around us.
5. Read about any daily happening in which the use of mathematics makes for a clearer understanding of the event. Explain why this is so.

▶ Motivations: specific topics in mathematics

TOPIC: **Understanding Money.** MOTIVATION: The United Nations and its agencies are in need of money for various activities. A contribution of 5¢ per child will help cure serious illness in backward areas around the world. "How much can this class contribute? What is the contribution of each nation of the world for the support of the United Nations?"

Tax figures: Utilize tax figures in the news to teach understanding of numbers in terms of dollars and cents, fundamentals involving money, and so forth. Utilize smaller figures such as sales tax per dollar for younger children, and larger figures such as those used in the nation's budget for older groups. For example: The President of the United States called for an outlay in a recent budget of about $98,000,000,000. This was $4,500,000,000 more than the previous year. The deficit for the year will be $11,900,000,000. Opponents of the budget wanted spending cuts of about $10,000,000,000.

For younger children, personal experiences involving the activities of children at home, in school and in the neighborhood should be used, e.g., purchasing candy for a class party, collecting milk money.

In general, utilize news items relating to: sales, wages, government spending, cost of living, foreign exchange, parents' sales receipts from grocery stores.

TOPIC: **Percent.** MOTIVATION: Discuss standard of living, cost of living, sales figures. "Eighty-eight percent of our families have washing machines; 67% have TV sets; 59% own cars. What percent of our population does not have each of these items? Forty percent of our population earn less than $5000. If our total population is 180,000,000, how many earn less than $5000?"

TOPIC: **Ratio and Proportion.** MOTIVATION: Utilize figures involving representation in our House of Representatives.

"In 1963 the proposed new United Arab Republic was to have a chamber of deputies based on proportional representation for 27,000,000 Egyptians, 4,000,000 Syrians, 7,000,000 Iraqi. What proportion of the total representation would each group have in the legislature?

"Lester B. Pearson was chosen Prime Minister of Canada in 1963. He won but was short of a majority vote. The liberals won 130 seats, the Conservatives 94 seats, the minor parties 41 seats. What proportion of the seats did each group win?"

Use newspaper articles relating to the batting averages of baseball players, rate of unemployment in the country, comparative changes in the cost of living indices.

TOPIC: **Decimal Fractions.** MOTIVATION: Use any article relating to money, prices, cost of living, budgets, trade, consumers, education, social security. "The price of sugar has gone up one tenth of a dollar. How much more will we pay?"

TOPIC: **Interest.** MOTIVATION: "How did the bank compute your interest this quarter? Why does the bank discourage you from withdrawing money in December? How does the bank compute your interest for the year?"

TOPIC: **Concept of Direction.** MOTIVATION: In teaching direction, discussions of trips of important personalities in the news will make the study of both the current topic and the mathematical concepts behind it more meaningful. Much of the news about nuclear testing and fall-out involves direction. For younger children, references should be made to class trips by groups in the neighborhood.

TOPIC: **Measurements.** MOTIVATION: Routes used by children and personalities in the news should be referred to: routes to school, to different cities, to parts of the world, to outer space. Analyzing movements of our nuclear air and sea craft, our Seventh Fleet, etc., involves an understanding of distances, direction, units of measure. An understanding of distance in terms of time and miles is necessary for an understanding of America and the danger spots in the world: Cuba, Laos, Viet Nam.

For younger children, the teacher should utilize current experiences involving arrangement of furniture in the room, location of points of interest in the school and in the neighborhood.

TOPIC: **Concepts of Time and Speed.** MOTIVATION: Utilize the following: a) the daily calendar, b) telling differences in time at various places in the world according to current news happenings all over the world, c) commemorating special events utilizing dates: Washington's Birthday, February 22, 1732. "How long ago was he born?"

TOPIC: **Graphs.** MOTIVATION: All newspapers, particularly the Sunday editions, have excellent charts and graphs which should be utilized at all times by teachers of mathematics. When necessary, figures may be edited to suit the needs and abilities of the class. Children should be asked to interpret graphs in the paper, or to make their own graphs based on figures showing changes in the cost of living, employment, membership in an international or national organization, population growth comparison studies, election returns, and so forth.

It should be noted in conclusion that all illustrations were taken from the newspaper; thus, the mathematics teacher must be well read in current events.

6

INTEGRATE LESSONS
WITH CURRENT AFFAIRS

► Social studies lessons and current affairs

Although with younger children in the primary grades, relating a holiday to past history is one of the simplest ways of introducing current events into the lesson, with older children, making a comparison between the past and the present is often more stimulating and more meaningful. For example, when teaching the American Revolution, some comparison might be made to revolutions going on today, in various parts of the world, of colonial peoples. In teaching the Articles of Confederation, the most likely parallel and comparison is the United Nations Charter.

A study of the Constitution of the United States or the government of the United States should never be made without the use of the daily newspaper. For example, in taking up the powers of Congress, children will not only get a better understanding of such powers, but a knowledge of current events, if, through newspaper headlines or pictures, they are led to see the relationships between their powers and current happenings.

Congress shall have the power to	Relationship to current happenings
tax	Income tax problem in the news
regulate post roads	Rising costs of postage stamps
raise an army	The draft laws
borrow money	United States bond issue
coin money	Study our coins and their inscriptions
punish counterfeiters	"T" men, TV programs
pass a law	Trace a current bill to its final stages

With the President in the news today, the study of the powers of

39

the President becomes meaningful when related to the actual activities of our executive as described in our paper:

Executive Powers	Newspaper Article
President's power to appoint	Cabinet members in the news
As Commander-in-chief	An international crisis
His treaty making power	Current international agreements
	Foreign officials visiting our President
His recommendations to Congress	Address to Congress and the people of the United States
His qualifications	Background of our present President

The following is a lesson where a current happening was integrated with a unit of work in the curriculum: "The Division of Powers between the Federal and State Government." [1]

1. Current Topic: President Johnson's State of the Union message.

2. Motivate both groups; the bright group and slow group, in a similar manner—that of a direct and personal approach. Two examples might be:

Will President Johnson's proposal for aid to education help you? Will his proposal for helping older people aid your grandparents?

3. Then why do some people claim that such federal aid could be considered improper or unconstitutional?

7th Year—Bright Group	7th Year—Slow Group
(Open text and interpretation of Article 1, Section 8, Amendment X of the Constitution)	
1. Class discussion	1. Teacher directed class discussion
2. Panel discussion	2. Filmstrips and motion pictures dealing with the powers of the federal government and those of the state government.
3. Debate: Pupils can debate parts of the President's program, such as the lowering of our tariff, federal aid to education, Medicare as it relates to the powers of the federal government vs. those of the state government or	3. Open textbook lesson on the role of the President in our government; relate to the State of the Union message; the powers of the federal government.
4. Special reports by the pupils: The powers of the federal government and those of the state government.	4. Have the students draw simple cartoons showing the various powers of the federal government and relate to the current topic of the day: the power of our federal government.

[1] Presented by Seymour Kazanowitz, Winthrop Junior High School, Brooklyn, N. Y.

Conclusions: Current legislation affecting our lives today has tended to:

a. increase the powers of our federal government. Explain.

b. State governments are still fighting to keep their state powers exclusively for themselves as in the case of the passage of "Civil Rights" bills. Explain.

Evaluation: Several methods which could be used to evaluate the work are:

1. Objective type test based on work discussed in class (more suitable for the bright group).

2. Oral questioning (for the slow and bright groups).

3. Composition or report based on the work (more suitable for the bright group).

4. Interpreting a cartoon which shows the powers of the federal government (for the slow group).

Even with children in the early childhood grades, we can take a current local issue and use it to develop an understanding of responsible citizenship. This lesson illustrates how it may be done:

DEVELOPING CONCEPTS

A worthwhile procedure relating the past to the present and the present to the past is to develop basic social studies concepts with the children. This will make social studies learning more meaningful and the reading of a newspaper more intelligible to our young people. Each period in history brings us a basic concept which can be applied to the world today:

Historical Event	Social Studies Concept	Its Effect on Us Today
American Colonial History	Subject Nationalities, Imperialism	Africa Today
Era of Good Feeling	Nationalism	France and Nuclear Weapons Growth of West Germany
Industrial Revolution 1816, post Civil War	Trends towards Economic Growth	Industrial Growth Today
Colonial Democracy	Developments of Democracy	Present Day Democratic Developments: Education, Social Security
Civil War	Sectionalism	Segregation Crisis
Washington's Foreign Policy	Isolation	NATO, U.N.
Hamilton's Tariff Policy Tariff of 1816	Tariff	Common Market

Thus, in teaching about a past event, children should learn a social studies concept which should be applied to a current situation, showing that this concept has existed through the ages.

▶ Science lessons and current events

Current events should be an integral part of every science lesson to make the subject more interesting, more vital, more real and more personal for our young people. In one daily newspaper, the following news items were found which could be used in science lessons:

Item	Unit of Work
Discrimination	Race, heredity
Weather notes: "World Weather Watch Approved"	Getting Acquainted with the World: the Earth and the Sun, Night and Day, Winds, Currents, etc.
"Liquor Licenses Investigated"	Health, Influences of Alcohol
Nuclear Testing	Our Atomic World; Radiation, Gases and their Properties
The NATO Atomic Force	Atomic Power
"Three of Four Valves in Heart Rebuilt"	Health and Prolonging Life Today
"Mother Catches Up in Red Cross Course in Health and Safety"	Health, Safety, Baby Care
"Smokers' Clinic Urged by Physicians"	Health; Cancer; Narcotics
"Bathyscaphe Arrives"	How Are Ships Submerged? Propelled? Nuclear Energy Used in Transportation

It can be seen, therefore, that within a given week, it is rare that current news items could not be correlated with work in the science class. Furthermore, classes often subscribe to science periodicals which enable the teacher to keep her science lessons up-to-date. For junior high school pupils, *Science News Letter* is an excellent weekly science newspaper published by the American Education Publication Corporation. *My Weekly Reader,* for younger children, has excellent current news items relating directly to science.

Here is a lesson in ninth year science where current news was used as the motivation and application step of the lesson.[2]

Aim: How to develop immunity

Motivation: How many of you have had colds this winter?

---

[2] Presented by Miss Ellen Shumsky, Winthrop Junior High School, Brooklyn, N. Y.

News Article: Twenty Different Cold Viruses Have Been Isolated

Development:

    I. Discuss the article: Why is it possible to get 20 different colds in one season?

       How can we develop immunity to colds?

       Why is it difficult to get immunity from colds?

    II. How many pupils have had a polio or smallpox vaccination? Why?

       How can vaccinations develop immunity to a specific disease?

       How are animals useful in giving us immunity? Student report on diphtheria.

Summary: Why can we immunize ourselves against smallpox? diphtheria? polio? Why is it more difficult to develop immunity of a similar kind from colds?

Application: Why do people who travel to the Far East take typhoid shots?

Enrichment: To which great scientists are we indebted for the concept of immunization? Student reports on Jenner, Pasteur, etc.

7

CURRENT EVENTS AS AN INDIVIDUAL SUBJECT

Current events may be brought into each lesson by correlating the work of the day with current happenings as described previously. Or, five minutes of each period, each day, could be devoted to discussing the highlights of the day. However, in addition, it is equally good teaching to devote one period a week to current events in order to tie together all the bits of current happenings mentioned during the week and/or to discuss in greater detail the important happenings of the week in the world around us.

▶ Giving the assignment

Assignments should be specific and limited to a few major topics for the period. In order to have intelligent class discussions or understandings, the class should have some apperceptive basis for understanding the current happening and all pupils should have done some reading on the given topics. The following are some procedures in making a current events assignment:

1. Where a weekly periodical is used in class, the teacher may use the key article as a basis for the current events lesson and thus give a "textbook" type of assignment. Should such periodicals arrive in class every Monday, the teacher and the class should spend five minutes to get a picture of the chief news of the week. The assignment for the current events lesson should be given for Friday of the week. This should include questions involving an understanding of the article in the periodical. In addition, this should include readings on the same topics in the newspapers of the week to get more detail and the latest developments in the news. Thus,

44

in brief, the weekly periodical becomes the guide for the teacher in assigning current events lessons. Such assignments are common in all grades from grade four through the high school years.

2. With younger children, in particular, current events become more real when they study famous personalities in the news. Thus with them, the teacher can assign two or three figures to be followed in the newspapers. Such personalities may include a national figure, an international figure, and a local figure. The pictures of such personalities should be posted on the current events bulletin board in advance. Children should be encouraged to make current events notebooks including such personalities. In the lower grades, this may become a "picture" book including pictures of the personality, map of the country he comes from and headlines about his work. The book may be divided into areas of the world and famous personalities in the news from such areas. This procedure can even be used with children in the first grade who learn to identify people in the news, especially at election time, and are asked to "match" similar pictures, or to watch television to see if they can recognize some of the faces. This, therefore, is the biographical approach to the study of current events, a very effective procedure with younger or "slow" pupils.

However, the procedure may be more advanced for use with older, more mature children. With the study of the various personalities in the news, the teacher may assign the following involving further reading, research, and evaluation:

> The background of the individual
> The problem confronting him
> His contributions to his country
> His contributions to the world
> The pupils' opinion of the individual

3. Where there is no weekly periodical, the assignment made by the teacher should be limited to a few topics. *It is poor teaching to ask the class to bring in any news they think is significant for the current events lesson.* This only results in a disorganized lesson where the pupils have no common basis for discussion and understanding of the current happening and the teacher cannot prepare her lesson properly in advance. Therefore, the teacher should by judicious selection guide the class to concentrate on

   a. Topic X in international affairs
   b. Topic Y in national affairs
   c. Topic Z in local affairs

For a current events lesson in language arts, the following procedures may be utilized:

    a. New books which were reviewed in the newspapers

    b. Review of plays or motion pictures

    c. Topics for discussion or debate or for oral reporting

For a current events lesson in science, the teacher may limit the areas to:

    a. General developments in science in the news this week

    b. Science developments relating to the human body

    c. Science developments relating to the earth and space

    d. Men of science in the news

For current events in art, the following areas may be assigned:

    a. Art personalities in the news

    b. Art shows in our city this week

    c. New developments in the field of: architecture, painting

For current events in music, the following specific areas may be assigned:

    a. Concerts given in our city this week

    b. Music personalities in the news

    c. Report on reviews of operas, operettas, musicals, musical productions

    d. Current reviews of new recordings

She should have the children answer the following types of basic questions:

    What the situation is?

    Why it occurred?

    Why it is important to us?

    What can we do about it?

    What is their opinion? Why?

4. With bright pupils, the teacher may make assignments which are broader in scope, using "specialist" committees to concentrate on particular areas in current affairs:

Class assignment: Three specific areas in current events, as indicated above. In addition, a committee of specialists may concentrate on a specific phase of current events as follows:

    a. A committee of four experts, each of whom is to present the major news in local, national, international affairs, and in special affairs, to be followed by class discussion. Or:

    b. Group 1: Read on the chief news of the week in local affairs

       Group 2: Read on chief news of the week in national affairs

       Group 3: European affairs

Group 4: Latin American affairs

Group 5: United Nations, etc.

Note: The teacher may decide on any area or topic she feels is important. For example, in an art class, Group 1: Special offerings by museums; Group 2: Artists in the news; Group 3: Special exhibits in the city; Group 4: Dress designs.

OR:

c. Special pupils or small committees may be assigned to interview political figures or other celebrities in the city, parents, teachers or other personalities on topics which are of current interest in the news.

5. For very young children, and for pupils with low reading scores, in order to enable them to read their weekly periodicals and newspapers more easily, the teacher may prepare rexographed material dealing with current events which can be used as part of an open-text lesson. However, these pupils should be using periodicals and newspapers together with such reading material in order to develop in them the habit of reading current news items.

▶ The textbook lesson

The simplest lesson to present is the textbook lesson based entirely on reading in a weekly periodical. This may follow the usual developmental lesson as used in most classes with stress on interpretation of pictures, headlines, charts, and the use of all types of teaching aids given in such weeklies. With slow groups and with younger children, the open-text lesson is always a good procedure for any area of study.

The following is a lesson plan utilizing the "textbook" procedure:

A CURRENT EVENTS PERIODICAL (SLOW AND BRIGHT GROUPS)

Topic for discussion: Struggle between United Nations Forces and Katangan Forces—reported in *World Week,* January 10, 1961. (Grade 9) [1]

Procedures for a Slow Group	Procedures for a Bright Group
A. Use *World Week* as an open textbook lesson.	A. The magazine *World Week* should be given to the class in advance with a homework assignment on the topic to be discussed, "The Congo."
B. Have the class interpret the picture on page 6.	
C. Have them read the bold print	

[1] Presented by Miss Lucille Kaplan, Winthrop Junior High School, Brooklyn, N. Y.

to get key ideas:

IN THE CONGO: CONFUSION AND CHAOS—SHARP STRUGGLE BETWEEN U.N. & KATANGA PROVINCE SIGNALS NEW TROUBLE

D. Teacher should write key names on the board:

Moishe Tshombe

Cyrille Adoula

By a pivotal question ask the children to tell who they are and why their names are mentioned.

E. One or two paragraphs at a time should be read always preceded by a thought question which directs the reading.

F. The teacher can diagram a simple cartoon to tell and illustrate a point and have the class interpret it.

G. Class should have a special section of the notebook divided into sections:

Who are they?

What are they?

Important events.

Under each section the class writes the name and the title of the person mentioned, the name of the city or an idea, and a single sentence summarizing the event. This should be copied from the board after the teacher has written it out as a summary of the discussion. Pictures of famous personalities and pictures cut out from the articles can be pasted in the notebook.

H. Vocabulary: At least two new words should be learned.

B. Panels, discussion groups or debating teams could be set up.

C. Class could be assigned to interview the man on the street for his opinions on the Congo crisis.

D. Special section in notebook similar to that of "slow" group. Class is expected to fill in each section as the discussions proceed and are responsible for illustrative materials.

E. Class could draw their own cartoons illustrating the points made.

F. Since this is a news item which represents a problem which is not easily resolved, groups could be assigned to follow it up as a unit.

G. Crossword puzzle, Republic of the Congo (page 24), can be assigned. This provides a very good summary of the contents of the article in *World Week*.

H. Filmstrip from *The New York Times* on the Congo as a follow up.

I. Procedures using research in encyclopedias: use of jot notes and reporting to get the history of the Congo.

J. If a long period of time is used, committees should be set up.

K. Use of articles, graphs, political cartoons and editorials from the newspaper. Pupils should be able to explain at least the headline and pictures relating to it.

L. Vocabulary: At least five new words should be learned.

The following points should be noted when teaching the open-text lesson to a "slow" class:

a. The class interprets pictures.

b. The class interprets key words and bold print.

c. Key names should be written on the board.

d. Reading of short paragraphs is always preceded by a directed reading question.

e. Where possible, the teacher should diagram a simple cartoon.

f. A record of their learning should be made in a notebook, such a record being simple and clear.

g. Vocabulary basic to understanding the current event should be stressed.

h. Children should learn at least two new words.

In teaching the "bright" group the following points should be noted:

a. An assignment should be given in advance.

b. Research work should be assigned for background and better understanding.

c. Special techniques should be utilized: interviews, debates, panel discussions.

d. Even with a bright group, cartoons and other visual aids may be utilized.

THE DISCUSSION METHOD: TEACHER LEADER

When the teacher assigns a limited number of specific topics and requests pupils to bring to class evidence of having read their assignment either by answering questions assigned or by bringing to class summaries of news items, the teacher can plan her lesson by providing a development of the key facts in the news, followed by discussions on the implications and importance of such news items to us. The following are samples of lessons prepared by teachers after assigning specific topics in the current news. The first lesson is based on a periodical not a newspaper.

▶ A current events periodical in a science lesson

Periodical: Science News Letter, March 23, 1963.[2]

Aim: How are some important materials obtained from earth?

Motivation: The United States is running low on some of its natural resources such as, coal, gold, silver, oil, etc. The *News Letter* has an article with the following heading: "Scientists Tap Volcanic-Like Water." We can get rich resources unknown to us today. Let us see how.

Development:

1. Read the first paragraph. Why is tapping volcanic-like water important to us?

---

[2] Presented by Miss Ellen Shumsky, Winthrop Junior High School, Brooklyn, N. Y.

2. How can we get gold and silver from this method? What are the advantages and disadvantages of this procedure?
3. What other methods are used to get gold? silver?

Medial Summary: Evaluate the various methods of getting gold and silver. Why are they all important?

4. In our daily living, we are dependent upon other materials which are found in the earth. What resources supply us with our fuel needs?

    a. Petroleum: How do we get petroleum from the earth? What is meant by distillation? fractional distillation? What relationship is there between drilling for oil and the discovery of volcanic-like water?

    b. Natural gas: Light the Bunsen burner. What is the nature of the fuel used here? How is it obtained? Discuss the origin of this fuel. What is the relationship of the study of natural gas to the article we are reading today?

    c. Coal: Have pupils report on coal mining referring to articles in the current papers relating to coal mining, its methods, the problems and dangers involved.

Summary: We get many of our sources of heat and energy from the earth. Discuss.

What methods are used to get the fuel resources from the earth?

How does this article explain how we can get other sources of heat and energy?

Why is it necessary to look for other means of getting energy? What other means of getting energy are the scientists working on today?

Homework: Special report on: Energy From the Sun, Energy From the Atom.

▶ A current events lesson for eighth year classes

Note: The plan for the "bright" group may be used, with modifications, for 9-12th year groups, language arts or social studies classes.

Topic: The President's Proposal for Federal Aid to Education.[3]

---

[3] Presented by Edward Blum, Winthrop Junior High School, Brooklyn, N. Y.

Slow Groups—8th year

Method: Much use of visual aids.

Motivation: Pictures of certain schools in the United States. One set of pictures showing old schools in certain poorer states in the union; another set of pictures of modern school buildings in wealthier states such as New York or California.

Questions:

1. What do these pictures tell you about the United States?
2. Why do you think certain states can provide more modern schools than other states?
3. Do you think that our federal government should provide aid to education in the United States? Why or why not?

Note: If an opaque projector is available, it should be used.

4. The teacher should also provide rexographed material for these students with the basic facts on the topic to be used in class discussion. On the bottom of each page, the teacher should have at least five questions as a basis for an open-text lesson.

Evaluation:

1. Informal: Observations of class discussions and pupil responses.
2. Checking of current events scrap books on articles dealing with federal aid to education. It is most important to check summaries below each article.
3. Informal Games: Three students interview another student, posing as the President of the United States and ask questions previously prepared by the entire class.

Note: Teacher checks the questions in advance and confers with the student who is to act as the "President," to check on his preparation.

Bright Groups—8th year

Assignment: Class to be arranged in two groups, A and B, to read newspapers on the topic: "Should the Federal Government Give Grants to Schools?" Group "A" should have the affirmative side, group "B," the negative.

Sources of information:
   a. *Times index*
   b. *Reader's Guide*
   c. Texts
   d. The Constitution of the United States
   e. Interviews

Method: After one week, a debate should be planned between the two groups, following an informal discussion in the class, where the teacher will list on the board the chief arguments presented by the pupils. These will be used as a basis for further research in preparation for the debate at a future date. Thus, the audience is prepared, and the debaters are given direction.

Evaluation:

Informal: Observations on class discussions and the debate.

Formal: Essay-type test "Do you agree or disagree with the President's proposal that the federal government give grants to the states for education? Give at least three concrete reasons to prove your position. For each example, explain where you received your information."

Aim: To present an overview of current happenings of the week in the world and in the nation in the field of literature and drama.

Content-outline:
1. New books published
2. New plays reviewed
3. Motion pictures reviewed
4. Interesting poems in the news
5. Unusual editorials in the news
6. Famous authors in the news

Procedure: Similar to the one used in the social studies lesson above.

AN OVERVIEW LESSON IN CURRENT EVENTS FOR A BRIGHT CLASS
IN ART, MUSIC, SCIENCE OR HOME ECONOMICS, GRADES 7-9

Aim: To present an overview of current happenings of the week in the world and in the nation in the field of art, music, science, home economics, etc.

Content-outline:
1. Famous men in the . . . . . area in the news
2. Important exhibits: art, music, scientific, fashion shows, food exhibits, etc.
3. Latest developments in the world of . . . . . at home and abroad.
4. Programs in the field of . . . . . on TV, radio
5. Latest books and periodicals

Procedure: Similar to the one used in the social studies lesson above.

DISCUSSION METHOD: SMALL GROUP DISCUSSIONS

The teacher could divide the class into five or six committees, each committee reading current articles on a specific topic. The pupils in each group get together in class for about ten minutes to pool information they read during the week on their given topic and then they choose a speaker to present their main ideas to the class after the committees are called back to their seats. These joint reports are then discussed by the class. Reminder to the teacher: Current topics assigned to groups should be rotated so that one week Group "A" will be assigned to local affairs. Or, Group "A" will report on a person in the news and Group "B" on an event in the news, etc., the assignment being reversed the following week. Another way to use the "small group" discussion idea is to assign no more than six topics to the entire class for their current events homework. On the day of the lesson, the teacher will use the 6-6-6 technique dividing the class into committees of six each, *each* committee pooling its information on one of the six given topics as above. When they reassemble, the teacher can conduct a class discussion or utilize pupil chairmen to lead the discussion on each of the six topics for the day.

▶ *A personality in the news*

Procedures with a bright class: 5-7th years. Any area of study.[4]

Aim: To become acquainted with a personality currently in the news. (Perhaps a head of state visiting the United States, a scientist, a famous musician, a well known artist, an outstanding writer, a person well known in the field of sports.) Why is "John Smith" so important in world affairs today?

Motivation: Our President is currently entertaining a famous person as his guest. If you had the opportunity to meet him and talk with him, what would you like to ask him about himself and his country?

Background Assignment: Divide the class into two groups, or select two small groups to have the following assignments:

Group 1: Assume that you are a newspaper reporter assigned to interview "John Smith," the President's current guest. What questions would you ask him about himself, his job, his country and his country's ideas on world affairs?

Group 2: Assume that you are a representative of "John Smith," the President's current guest. Find out all you can about him, his job, his country, and his country's ideas about world affairs.

Both groups should use magazine and newspaper articles for information and also be made aware of any television programs that might interview or discuss the person.

Materials: Map with country of person clearly visible. Pictures of the person or representative scenes of his country or ideas.

Development: Reintroduction and motivation by the teacher: Today the spotlight falls on the country of X (illustrated with map and pictures), whose distinguished citizen, "John Smith," is currently visiting our country. We are privileged to have some of his representatives with us here today.

---

[4] Presented by Miss Gilda Scharf, P.S. 175, Brooklyn, N. Y.

Directed Listening: Draw three columns on a sheet of paper. Label the columns: "The Country," "The Person," "Ideas." Classify each item you hear into one of these groups by placing the main idea in the appropriate column.

Questions and Answers: by the assigned group, and then, if the entire class is not participating, questions by the rest of the class.

Summary: directed by the teacher and the class to review the role of the person in his country's affairs or in his special area of work. The class at this time can refer to their recorded notes, the by-product of their directed listening.

Outcomes: Developing an interest in important people revealing facts about their country and their contribution to the world.

Awakening an interest in reading biographies.

Increasing knowledge of foreign countries and their contributions to the world.

Developing skills in organizing an interview.

Doing research for specific data.

Training in skills in understanding facts and then drawing conclusions and generalizations from them.

A LESSON INVOLVING CURRENT EVENTS
AND TRAINING IN RESEARCH: GRADES 5-9,
LANGUAGE ARTS CLASS [5]

Aim: Why is it that the Congo features in the news with Belgium when these two countries are so far apart geographically?

Motivation: Display of newspaper clippings with material on African affairs featuring news about the Congo and Belgium.

Materials:

1. A one volume encyclopedia
2. One volume from a many volume set of encyclopedias
3. Brochures
4. Yearly supplements
5. Rexographed work sheets

Procedure: Elicit answers to:

1. To what book do we usually turn for a brief, concise bit of information?
2. What are the standards for a good encyclopedia?
3. What are good research procedures? Teach good research procedures:

---

[5] Presented by Miss Lucille Kaplan, Winthrop Junior High School, Brooklyn, N. Y.

a. Read the article through completely.

b. Reread and take jot notes.

c. Consult other books.

d. Later on, write a report in essay form or in outline form or on 3 x 5 cards for oral reporting.

e. Check work by rereading finished report.

Assignment: Bring in a report on the Belgian Congo to be delivered in class (based on research during library lesson).

THE PICTURE LESSON

For young children, and for children with low reading scores, it again should be stressed that the use of pictures and concrete materials is very important to make current events meaningful. Here the bulletin board, the flannel board, the pictures in the weekly periodical or in other magazines are basic to the lesson. Where the children do not provide the teacher with adequate illustrative material, the teacher should be prepared to have her own.

A. Pictures of personalities in the news: identification, importance.

B. Pictures of places in the news: identification, importance.

C. Learning by interpretation of cartoons. The cartoons may be presented by means of reproduction, the opaque projector, diagrams of the cartoons or brief explanations of the cartoon:

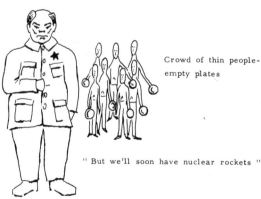

Crowd of thin people—empty plates

" But we'll soon have nuclear rockets "

Questions:

1. Who is the man on the left?

2. Whom do the people represent?

3. What story does the cartoon tell?

4. What point is the cartoonist making?

5. What did you learn from the cartoon?

D. Give a brief description of the cartoon: "What would you

55

learn about the problems of our present administration from the following cartoon?" "The U.S. economy is represented by a rowboat sailing a stormy sea. The words are labeled, "High Cost of Living" and "Unemployment." The oarsman of this unsteady boat is President Johnson. Title: "Will He Make It?" What other suggestions for cartoons do you have? Draw them.

E. Interpreting a map or a series of maps: "Germany—Key to the Cold War in Central Europe," *New York Times,* November 12, 1961. Colorful maps make current events alive when properly used. Teachers should utilize *The New York Times* services for reproductions of maps in the *Times.*

F. Interpretation of graphs, charts, etc. (Excellent for mathematics lessons.)

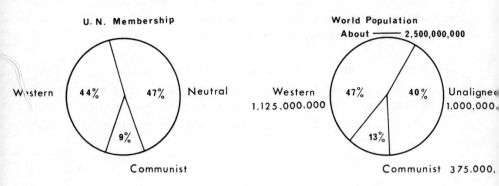

U. N. Membership

Western 44% 47% Neutral 9% Communist

World Population
About ———— 2,500,000,000

Western 1,125,000,000 47% 40% Unaligned 1,000,000 13% Communist 375,000,

Questions:

Chart on United Nations Membership

1. Why are the neutral powers important in the United Nations?

2. If the Western Bloc has 44% of the votes in the United Nations, why is it worried about Communist domination?

3. Why do both the Western Bloc and the Communist Bloc have a great interest in the neutral group.

4. What is the relationship between the two groups?

5. Why can it be said that the unaligned people of the world hold the balance of power?

6. Why is it of great concern to the Western nations to win over the people of the unaligned nations?

Where a teacher does not prefer to set aside a full period a week for current events she may use another procedure: The Five Minute Daily Report. Each day, a different current happening should be taken up for five minutes: Monday: A domestic event; Tuesday: a local event; Wednesday: an event in the Far East, etc. Or: Monday—a personality; Tuesday—an event; Wednesday—a book review; Thursday—a TV or radio review, etc.

8

HOW TO TEST
AND EVALUATE CURRENT
EVENTS LEARNING

▶ General rules for testing in social studies

Every test should include questions relating to a current situation. For example, if the class were studying the Policy of Isolation or the Monroe Doctrine, a unit test might include a current question relating to this topic on U.S.S.R.'s intervention in Cuba, the membership of the United States in the North Atlantic Treaty Organization, the policy and membership of the United States in the Organization of American States, the policy of the United States during the various political crises in Latin America today, etc. If the class has just concluded the study of the period of explorations and discoveries during the fifteenth and sixteenth centuries, a testing program should also include travels and explorations into space, current events relating to the North and South Poles and explorations into unknown parts of Africa and Asia. The development of American civil rights during colonial days should be evaluated along with current happenings involving freedom of speech and press, the right to assemble, the right of Congress to tax, trial by jury and the use of the fifth amendment. Finally, the story of history always included the story of wars which have causal factors and results often similar to more recent wars and revolutions in modern times.

In most schools, the study of famous American documents is taken up beginning with the fifth year. Such documents usually include: the Constitution of the United States, the Declaration of Independence, features of city and state constitutions and the

Charter of the United Nations. A testing program should not merely have children quote or list facts from such documents. Such facts are meaningless unless children can apply them to real situations existing today. For example, in a high school class, it is not sufficient for children to explain the meaning of "reserved powers," "delegated powers" or "implied powers." Pupils should be able to give examples of such powers from our own lives today. Even with youngsters in the fifth year and through the junior high school grades, such application of principles should be tested: "What are the powers of the President of the United States? Give examples from current situations showing how he utilizes such powers."

Children from the first year through the twelfth year should be responsible for being able to identify people, places or events.

Teachers of geography, from the kindergarten through the senior year in high school, should never test geographical facts in isolation. For example, in the primary grades, pupils may be tested to see that they understand that the events which took place around them were "near or far," as related to distance from their home, or "east, south, north or west" in relationship to the school.

With older children beginning with grade seven, and with brighter pupils in grade six, teachers should provide a testing program where they can provide historical background to many current happenings: What is the relationship of the present desegregation movement to Amendment 13? The Reconstruction Period?

Finally, no testing program in current events should exclude the evaluation of pupils' ability to understand the meaning of basic social studies terms in the news. Tests even for children in the primary grades should include vocabulary questions to enable our young people to develop a basic understanding of current political and economic events.

▶ General rules for testing in language arts

Comparisons should be made of figures in novels and story books with current personalities in the news or in current literature or drama.

Pupils should be responsible for being able to identify dramatists, plays, plots and authors who are in the news in our literary world.

The teacher of English should avail herself of the opportunity to test for attitudes and judgments utilizing current happenings.

Even grammatical errors and the proper use of words can be

tested by utilizing sentences taken from our current newspapers and periodicals.

▶ General guide for testing in mathematics

Examples and problems can be based on real situations.

Fundamental processes can be tested by utilizing figures relating to population, taxation, unemployment, prices, distance, membership in national or international organizations, votes, etc.

Newspapers always carry excellent charts, diagrams and other visual aids which can be used to test for an understanding of number concepts, dollars and cents, fractions, percentage, graphs, size and shape and other units in mathematics.

In all subject areas, there should be an evaluation of reading comprehension. Nothing is as real and as meaningful as the evaluation of the understanding of newspaper clippings and headlines, pictures, cartoons and charts.

▶ Informal evaluation procedures

The Current Events Notebook:

All children can keep a current events notebook which will suit the age and abilities of youngsters from the earliest grade through senior high school. Primary grade pupils should have a picture notebook. This might include a cooperative class story of "what happened in the news."

CURRENT EVENTS NOTEBOOK—SOCIAL STUDIES [1]
Sept. 19— to June 19—

Note: The notebook will be divided into sections, as indicated below:

Section I

Current Events: General

Our City and State	Miscellaneous News
National News	Sports News
Washington News	Science in the News
European News	Music in the News
African News	The Arts

For each area, the following sub-topics or questions will be set up:
1. Who are they? Name, title, picture
2. What are they? Names of bureaus, agencies, etc.

---

[1] Presented by Miss Marian Knapp, Winthrop Junior High School, Brooklyn, N. Y.

3. Related social studies topic studied in class, illustrated where possible.
4. Learning from maps: Use pictures, maps from newspapers: Geographic concepts, National affairs, Economic affairs, Projections.

Section II

Word Study: Social Studies Terms We Learned from the News.

Section III

Areas of the World: Current Affairs Organized under Geographic Areas.

Europe	South America
The Middle East	Canada
The Far Eeast	Australia
Africa	

Include the following:

1. Basic facts	5. Pictures
2. Original illustrations	6. Summarized clippings
3. Cartoons	7. Headlines
4. Maps	

Section IV

We Show Progress: Tests Which Were Marked and Corrected During the Term.

A CURRENT EVENTS NOTEBOOK IN MUSIC
Current Happenings in the Field of Music
Sept. 19—   June 19—

Section I

General news events involving music in: Our City and State, Our Country, Our Hemisphere, The World.

Current Events in the World of Music, Concerts, Musicales, Operettas, Operas, Music and Dance Events, Famous Personalities.

For each topic, the following questions should be answered:

What is it? Title, picture
Where is it taking place?
What are the important selections?
Who are the important people involved?
What did the critics say about it?

Answers may take the form of written statements, pictures or newspaper clippings and headlines.

Section II

Latest recordings: classical
                    operatic
                    folk songs
                    popular
Latest books on music and musicians, TV programs

Section III

Word Study: New names we learned in the news
            Musical terms in the news

Section IV

Current topics related to our units of study.

Unit of Study	Current News Items
Folk Songs	Joan Baez Performs

When a teacher uses the current events notebook in her class, it should be collected periodically and marked by the teacher. Caution should be taken so that, to insure fair and most valid evaluation, greater weight be given to content rather than to artistic talent in preparation of such a notebook.

Appraisal of Pupil Projects

Especially with the younger pupils, the teacher can evaluate learning by appraising actual projects children make to apply their knowledge of current affairs to creative and concrete activities: They can construct paper cut-out symbols to represent specific events; they may dramatize an important happening; they may keep an ongoing record of the progress of a significant situation; they may make dioramas; they may be asked to identify signs, symbols, pictures; they may make a diagrammatic map of a local neighborhood, city, state or country to identify the location of a current happening. Young children can use blocks, sand tables and other "play" material to describe what they learn.

Current Events Homework

Another method of informal evaluation of current events learnings involves careful checking of homework.

Homework can take the form of:

a. Reports

b. Answers to specific questions as drawn up by the teacher or questions which are found in current events periodicals, special student editions of newspapers or Sunday supplements.

c. Clippings which are properly summarized or underlined by pupils.

d. Preparation of the weekly current events bulletin board by rotating squads of pupils.

Games and Contests

A very interesting and enjoyable procedure for evaluating current events learning is by the use of games, contests, and dramatizations. There are many radio and TV programs which can give the teacher of any class, on all levels, ideas for testing the class: "Person to Person" interviews, "You Are There" programs, "Meet the Press," "Tic Tac Dough," "You Don't Say," etc. In addition, there is always the old and true "Current Events Bee" where the class is divided into two teams with the winning team receiving additional credit awards. Questions for such a contest should be drawn up by pupils, who must also provide correct answers to them. To get a good variety of questions, it is advisable to assign a different area to each row or group: questions on national affairs, European events, cultural events, local affairs, sports events, etc. The teacher, of course, should screen these questions carefully and select the ones that help to achieve the goals of current events instruction.

Teacher's Daily Observations

As an aid to evaluation, teachers should make careful note of the interest of the pupils in current events, their contributions to discussions and their applications of understanding of basic factors and concepts to items of current interest.

► Formal evaluation procedures

Since written testing is an integral part of our teaching program, provision should be made for such evaluations for all pupils beyond the third grade. Sources for such tests, as previously indicated, may come from periodicals or newspapers, and notes and outlines which were developed during classroom recitations. The teacher should usually prepare the questions, but the preparation of questions, short answer and essay, by pupils is also desirable. Such pupil activity is often in itself a good indication of how well children interpret and understand current events. These written tests should have all types of questions: short answer, essay, and tests of reading interpretation. Reading interpretation questions should include the interpretation of pictures, cartoons, and graphs. Among the types of short answer questions which lend themselves extremely well to testing of current events are the following:

1. Test of personalities in the news: *Who Am I?* I was born in Massachusetts; I ran for President of the United States in 1960. Who am I?

2. Test of personalities in the news: *Matching question*

   Column A   Column B
   Personality   His position or his contribution

3. Test of personalities in the news: *Identification of pictures.* (Good for younger children or poor readers.)

4. Geography questions: Interpretation of a map as it relates to current events.
5. Chronological Order Question:
   a. *Which event came first?* (Good for younger children.)
   b. *Arrange the following three events in chronological order.* (Good for older pupils.)
6. Matching questions showing causal relationships

Column A	*Column B*
Causes	Results

7. Testing vocabulary: The matching question:

Column A	*Column B*
Word or term	Definition

After completing a unit of work, teachers should provide essay questions. Such questions might be of the following types:

a. A question which is directly integrated with the unit being tested.
b. An essay devoted solely to testing current events learnings.
c. An extra-credit question dealing chiefly with current events.

Specific examples and suggestions in drawing up various types of questions can be found in Lillian C. Howitt's *Practical Classroom Testing,* Part II, Prentice-Hall, Inc. (Englewood Cliffs, 1961).

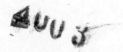